DATE DUE

PRINTED IN U.S.A.

AMERICAN VALUES AND FREEDOMS

THE RIGHT TO BEAR ARMS

by **DUCHESS HARRIS, JD, PHD** with Rebecca Morris

Essential Library

An Imprint of Abdo Publishing | abdopublishing.com

ABDOPUBLISHING.COM

Published by Abdo Publishing, a division of ABDO, PO Box 398166,
Minneapolis, Minnesota 55439. Copyright © 2018 by Abdo Consulting Group,
Inc. International copyrights reserved in all countries. No part of this book
may be reproduced in any form without written permission from the publisher.
Essential Library™ is a trademark and logo of Abdo Publishing.

Printed in the United States of America, North Mankato, Minnesota
102017
012018

Interior Photos: Steve Oehlenschlager/iStockphoto, 4–5; Paul Moody/
iStockphoto, 9; Keith Homan/Shutterstock Images, 12; Charles Haire/
Shutterstock Images, 13; Ryan Rodrick Beiler/Shutterstock Images, 14;
Kevin M. McCarthy/Shutterstock Images, 16–17, 24; Vitalii Gaidukov/
Shutterstock Images, 19 (top); James A. Boardman/Shutterstock Images,
19 (bottom); Everett Historical/Shutterstock Images, 26–27, 31, 34, 39;
Curtis Compton/Atlanta Journal-Constitution/AP Images, 36–37; Christopher
Halloran/Shutterstock Images, 44; Saul Loeb/AFP/Getty Images, 46; Donald
Uhrbrock/The LIFE Images Collection/Getty Images, 48; AP Images, 50,
81; Noel Davis/Atlanta Journal-Constitution/AP Images, 52; San Francisco
Examiner/AP Images, 54; Dennis Cook/AP Images, 58–59; Ira Schwartz/
AP Images, 60; iStockphoto, 67; Jose Luis Magana/AP Images, 68–69; Josh
Reynolds/AP Images, 72; Lukas Maverick Greyson/Shutterstock Images, 75;
Evan Vucci/AP Images, 76; Carolyn Kaster/AP Images, 78; Splash News/
Newscom, 83; Grace Beahm-Pool/Getty Images News/Getty Images, 86;
Shutterstock Images, 90–91; David Mbiyu/Shutterstock Images, 93; Eugene
Hoshiko/AP Images, 96

Editor: Patrick Donnelly
Series Designer: Becky Daum

Publisher's Cataloging-in-Publication Data

Names: Harris, Duchess, author. | Morris, Rebecca, author.
Title: The right to bear arms / by Duchess Harris and Rebecca Morris.
Description: Minneapolis, Minnesota : Abdo Publishing, 2018. | Series:
        American values and freedoms | Online resources and index.
Identifiers: LCCN 2017946727 | ISBN 9781532113024 (lib.bdg.) | ISBN
        9781532151903 (ebook)
Subjects: LCSH: Firearms–Law and legislation–Juvenile literature. | Gun
        control–United States– Juvenile literature. | Constitutional law–United
        States–Juvenile literature.
Classification: DDC 344.730533–dc23
LC record available at https://lccn.loc.gov/2017946727

CONTENTS

CHAPTER 1

DIFFERENT PERSPECTIVES

For many Americans, hunting is a family
tradition and bonding activity.

The Second Amendment of the US Constitution guarantees
American citizens the right to bear arms. What that means,
however, is open to interpretation. It seems there are almost
as many ways to view that right as there are people in
the country.

A HUNTING PERSPECTIVE

Forrest Burris grew up surrounded by the hunting culture of
rural Mississippi. His grandfather was a hunter, his father
was a hunter, and by the age of ten, Forrest was

carrying his own rifle on hunts. He started hunting by himself at 11, and he shot a deer for his first kill when he was 12. Burris remembers those early trips fondly. In addition to bonding with family and friends, he enjoyed "just sitting out there and watching all the wildlife—watching the sun hit the trees. I liked that so much I didn't even care if I got a deer."[1]

People choose to hunt for a variety of reasons. They may have an interest in obtaining food naturally; they may support hunting's connection to conservation and environmentalism; or, like Burris, they may come from a culture or family with a tradition of hunting. For those with deep roots in the tradition, the equipment involved in hunting—guns included—often holds special sentimental value. Many of the guns Burris owns came from his grandfather, and he anticipates passing them on to his own son one day.

Larry Schweiger, the former president of the National Wildlife Federation, has a similar emotional attachment to his guns. Schweiger remembers the day his father handed down the heirlooms:

> *Passing those guns to me was important in our family. For hunters, it's all kind of wrapped up together— firearms, keeping them in good working order, bonding and the people you hunt with. The ritual of where you go, conservation attitudes and respect for animals. . . . It's deeply ingrained in life.*[2]

THE SECOND AMENDMENT

The right to bear arms appears in the Second Amendment of the US Constitution: "A well regulated Militia, being necessary to the security of a free State, the right of the people to keep and bear Arms, shall not be infringed."[3] It is a relatively short statement, just 27 words long, ratified in 1791 with the other nine amendments that make up the Constitution's Bill of Rights.

Despite its short length, the Second Amendment has received much scrutiny over its wording. Some interpretations focus on the second half of the amendment to claim that arms access is a basic right for each individual citizen. In this view, individuals can exercise their right to bear arms for a wide range of purposes. Other interpretations focus on the first part of the amendment, which places arms rights in the context of a well-regulated militia. These interpretations argue that the right to bear arms is a collective right for the safety and protection of Americans as a group.

Additionally, people debate the meaning behind specific words in the amendment. For example, *arms* has a different meaning today than it did in the 1700s. In the past, some laws grouped guns with other kinds of arms, such as knives and daggers. However, as technology has changed, so have understandings of the term *arms*. In a 2016 case, for example, courts debated whether stun guns qualified as "arms" that people have a right to carry. Other frequently debated terms include *state, people,* and *keep and bear.*

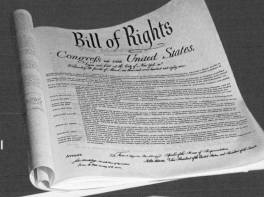

The right to bear arms is guaranteed by the Second Amendment of the Bill of Rights.

Citizens protested gun violence against African Americans in Chicago, Illinois, in 2016.

Committed hunters such as Burris and Schweiger view guns as tools of their craft that must be properly handled, maintained, and understood. Hunters learn gun safety at an early age, often from family or community members. Many states also require hunters to take an education course, which typically includes a firearms safety component. New hunters usually have to show proof of successfully completing the course before they are allowed to obtain the license needed to hunt legally. "I think sportsmen have a unique understanding of responsible firearms use," says Colorado hunter Gaspar Perricone. "It's something most of us take great pride in."[4]

A PERSPECTIVE OF A COMMUNITY IN DANGER

The city of Chicago often receives attention for its high rates of gun violence. In 2016, there were more than 700 homicides involving firearms reported.[5] It was the highest number of homicides in any major US city that year, and the most in Chicago since 1998. Growing up in the area, Kyisha Weekly experienced the effects of gun violence. One summer night when Weekly was a young teenager, a friend was killed in a drive-by shooting while hanging out with other friends. At the time, police suspected the shooting was related to gang activity even though the victim was not involved with a gang. A few years later, another girl Weekly knew was shot and killed by a peer after arguing with that person about a relationship with a boy. Weekly's brother and nephew also died from gun violence. Witnessing gun violence has affected nearly every aspect of Weekly's life. She rarely takes her young daughter outside to play or for casual walks, and she worries about simple, everyday tasks such as waiting at the bus stop. "People [are] getting shot," she says. "It's out of control."[6]

BREAKING THE CYCLE OF GUN VIOLENCE

Several of the points in Cook County Commissioner Richard Boykin's plan to reduce the number of shootings in Chicago focus on addressing the root causes that underlie urban gun violence. The proposed ideas include parenting workshops, job training programs, curfews, and changes to how drug offenses and addictions are handled in the legal system. The plan also includes strict penalties and legal action against people possessing guns illegally and those involved in planning or executing a shooting. However, Boykin believes that without addressing root causes of violent gun use, those harsher penalties would do little to reduce the cycle of gun-related crimes, injuries, and deaths in Chicago and other urban areas.

In response to another Chicago shooting in 2016, Cook County Commissioner Richard Boykin used sharp language to describe the problem: "The communities most heavily impacted by gun violence in the City of Chicago are nothing short of war zones, and just as in the other war-torn regions of the world, our children are not safe."[7] Boykin was referring specifically to the death of Demarco Webster Jr., an honors student killed by a stray bullet while he was helping his father load a car. To reduce gun activity, Boykin proposed a seven-point plan, including harsher penalties for illegal gun possession. Boykin has also advocated for legislative changes and community initiatives to fight the negative impact of guns in the community he serves.

A SELF-DEFENSE PERSPECTIVE

Sarah McKinley, a recently widowed young mother, was at home alone with her infant son in a rural area of Oklahoma on December 31, 2011, when two men tried to break into her home. McKinley pushed a sofa in front of the door to block it, placed her son in his crib, called 911, and readied two guns out of fear that the men would force their way inside before the police arrived. One of them broke through the barricade with a knife in his hand. McKinley shot and killed him. Police determined that McKinley had used her gun legally to protect herself and her son. McKinley said that using her weapon against someone is "not something I ever wanted to do," but that it was a

CASTLE DOCTRINE

Laws that permit self-defense inside one's home have a special term associated with them: *Castle Doctrine*. The term comes from the expression "a man's home is his castle." The expression means that people should be able to feel secure and should be able to have control in their homes. Castle Doctrines vary from state to state, but they generally allow people to use force, even deadly force, if they fear bodily harm or criminal activity by an intruder. Often, a Castle Doctrine specifies that the property owner shouldn't have to retreat. Sometimes these laws apply to vehicles and workplace settings as well.

step she had to take when confronted by a man with a deadly weapon. "I chose my son," McKinley said.[8]

McKinley's case received news coverage because it was a particularly dramatic incident that resulted in a death. Proponents of keeping guns on hand for protection argue that there are also many quieter incidents in which would-be attackers flee at the mere sight of a gun raised in defense. "Are criminals afraid of a law-abiding citizen with a gun?" one law enforcement officer asked rhetorically in a note to researcher John Lotts, who studies gun usage. "You bet."[9] To support his point, the officer gives an example of a 70-year-old woman who was able to frighten away a man attempting to break into her home. When she heard him trying to kick down the door, she pulled back the curtain of her window to show that she had a weapon. The man fled immediately. In 2013, a survey by the Pew Research Center and a poll by Gallup both revealed that protection was the most commonly expressed reason for owning a gun.[10]

Firearms are often sold at gun shows.

A SUICIDE PERSPECTIVE

On March 4, 2015, 13-year-old Cayman Naib, who lived just outside of Philadelphia in Newton Square, Pennsylvania, received an e-mail from his school, noting that he was in danger of failing one of his classes. Cayman took a gun from his family's home, walked through their wooded yard to a remote creek, and shot himself. He died from the bullet wound to his head. Cayman's family says the suicide happened within 20 to 30 minutes of receiving the upsetting news about his schoolwork.[11]

Gunshots are often a fast and highly lethal method of suicide, and they are the manner of death in approximately one-half of all suicides in the United States.[12] Furthermore, suicides, not homicides, account for the majority of the nation's gun deaths. In a report published by the Centers for Disease Control and Prevention (CDC), of the 33,594 firearm deaths in 2014, 63.7 percent were suicides, while 32.8 percent were homicides.[13] That statistic is part of an ongoing pattern, and suicides consistently account for more deaths than homicides. Suicide is a serious concern in the United States, where it is the tenth-leading cause of death overall.[14] It is the second-leading cause of death among young people (from the ages of 10 to 34).[15]

Researchers point out that suicide is often an impulsive action. Guns allow people caught in a desperate moment to act quickly on their desperation. Cayman's family agrees with that observation, as does Karyl Beal, whose daughter Arlyn also committed suicide with a gun. "People have told us that if Arlyn had not taken the gun, she could have killed herself another way." Beal admits, "That's possible." However, she continues, "It's also possible that the delay as she looked for another way would have given her mind time to move out of the suicidal trance she was in at the moment. That lost opportunity took away our chance to help and save her."[16]

A DEBATE: PAST, PRESENT, AND FUTURE

The perspectives above represent only a few of the many positions people take on the right to bear arms in the United States. National events such as wars, the country's geographic expansion, prominent assassinations, social movements,

Progun activists counterprotest at the Million Mom March, a major gun-safety rally in Washington, DC, in 2000.

14

mass shootings, and court cases have influenced opinions and increased discussion surrounding arms and the people's right to them.

American citizens have debated, often passionately, who should be allowed to carry weapons and who should not, what kinds of weapons may be available, and how this right to bear arms fits in alongside other national rights. People question the founders' intent in creating the Second Amendment. They debate its limits, the meaning of the phrase "well regulated Militia," and whether the amendment—now more than 200 years old—is outdated. The debate is ongoing, but it's impossible to deny the impact guns continue to have on American society.

DISCUSSION STARTERS

- In addition to the four perspectives presented in this chapter, what are other reasons people may feel strongly in favor of or opposed to guns?

- Is there a difference between the unalienable rights listed in the Declaration of Independence (life, liberty, and the pursuit of happiness) and the rights listed in the Constitution such as the right to bear arms, the right to free speech, and the right to a fair trial?

- The right to bear arms is one of the United States' most controversial rights. Why do people feel so passionately about this right?

CHAPTER 2

ARMING A NEW NATION

Reenactors recreate famous battles from the Revolutionary War.

Firearms have a storied place in iconic moments of the nation's founding. Ralph Waldo Emerson's poem "Concord Hymn" memorializes the initial gunfire of the American Revolution (1775–1783) as "the shot heard round the world."[1] The war's first battles took place at Lexington and Concord in Massachusetts on April 19, 1775. During those battles, minutemen took up their arms against the British troops, called regulars. The minutemen had caught wind of the regulars' objectives to strip them of the power to rebel. Those objectives included confiscating the colonists' gunpowder as well as capturing colonial leaders Samuel Adams and John Hancock. En route, the regulars first encountered the minutemen at Lexington, where the British leader Major John Pitcairn is said to have ordered, "Lay down your arms, you damned rebels."[2]

The minutemen did not give up their arms. One of the reasons they had assembled was to stop the British pillage of their armories. The colonists viewed being disarmed as an attempt to stifle their resistance and subjugate them to British governance. The battles of Lexington and Concord showed the colonists were willing to fight in order to protect their access to arms. Such events have transformed arms into symbols of American freedom. However, arms also have a complex history that extends beyond this symbolism. This complexity was evident in the process of writing and passing the Second Amendment as well as in the long national history of arms control and regulations.

WRITING THE RIGHT TO BEAR ARMS

Once the colonists achieved independence, they faced the task of organizing a national government. Until 1787, the new nation abided by the Articles of Confederation, but it soon became clear the country needed a document that outlined the rights of the people and the duties of the central government. State delegates convened to draft the US Constitution. Along with several other issues, the right to bear arms was the subject of much debate and discussion among the delegates. Delegates agreed that there was an important connection between access to arms and maintaining liberty against tyrannical forces. British attempts at disarmament had been serious provocations in the events leading up to the Revolutionary War.

Firearms used in the past are very different from the firearms available today.

However, delegates had different opinions about the extent of the right to bear arms and how best to preserve it.

By the time of the Constitutional Convention in 1787, several states had already written up their own constitutions and declarations of rights, which included provisions about arms and who could bear them. For example, the Virginia declaration of rights (1776) stated that "a well-regulated militia, composed of the body of the people, trained to arms, is the proper, natural, and safe defense of a free state."[3] The declaration of rights in the Massachusetts constitution contained more direct wording about the right to bear arms. It asserted, "The people have a right to keep and to bear arms for the common defense."[4] Alongside these proclamations of arms rights, states worried about leaving weapons in the hands of standing armies controlled by a central government. Permanent standing armies had the potential to threaten the liberty of the people. Both Virginia and Massachusetts, as well as other states, declared that it was dangerous for the central government to maintain and control standing armies in times of peace. Delegates brought the opinions of their states with them as they discussed how to include arms rights in the national Constitution.

During those discussions, delegates tended to fall into two camps: the Federalists and the Anti-Federalists. Anti-Federalists were distrustful of a strong central government. They objected to parts of the Constitution that allowed for a standing army and put the state militias under the control of the federal government. They also wanted to see language forbidding the government to disarm individual citizens.

The Anti-Federalists advocated for a bill of rights that would protect individual liberties and strengthen checks and balances on the central government. Abuse of personal liberties by the powerful British monarchy weighed heavily in the Anti-Federalist point of view.

Meanwhile, the Federalists believed that a strong central government was the best way to ensure

DRAFTS AND REVISIONS

The wording that stands in the Second Amendment today passed through rounds of drafting and revisions before it was adopted by lawmakers. James Madison originally proposed the amendment as: "The right of the people to keep and bear arms shall not be infringed; a well armed and well regulated militia being the best security of a free country: but no person religiously scrupulous of bearing arms shall be compelled to render military service in person." The mention of religion was intended to protect those such as Quakers whose religious beliefs did not align with bearing arms. Delegates pointed out that the wording could lead an oppressive government to decide arbitrarily whether a person was religiously scrupulous and thus take their arms away. States' rights activists also advocated for the change of wording from "free country" to "free State."[5]

efficient functioning in the country and to protect individuals. Federalists believed that the Constitution provided sufficient checks and balances without a bill of rights. They claimed that a bill of rights was unnecessary and that it could in fact be harmful, rather than helpful, to list individual liberties because no document could ever possibly "enumerate all the rights of men."[6] As a compromise, the Constitution was adopted in 1789 with the condition that amendments, including the right to bear arms, would be added later. In 1791, the required number of states had ratified the Bill of Rights, and it officially became a legal part of the Constitution. At the time, the Bill of Rights comprised ten amendments. The second of these read: "A well regulated Militia, being necessary to the security of a free State, the right of the people to keep and bear Arms, shall not be infringed."

REGULATING THE RIGHT TO BEAR ARMS

As they discussed the right to bear arms, legislators in the new country were also enacting laws that regulated arms use for a variety of reasons, including civic responsibility and public safety. Even during the Revolution, several states passed laws that required people to pledge allegiance to the United States. If they did not do so, the state would seize their arms and

The types of guns designed for military service in the 1700s differed from the types of guns most colonists owned for personal use. Colonists often owned lighter firearms used for hunting and pest control rather than the heavier arms designed for battle. As a result, states sometimes required militiamen to purchase military-style weapons, or the states provided them with those types of weapons. The capabilities of different kinds of firearms have been an important point of debate, currently and historically, among gun rights advocates and gun control advocates. Certain kinds of guns and ammunition are more powerful and more damaging than other kinds. For example, an assault weapons ban provoked strong reactions in 1994. It sought to prevent the general public from purchasing powerful, high-capacity weapons originally created for military purposes rather than hunting or sporting purposes.

ammunition in order to thwart opposition from British loyalists. Arms regulations worked to ensure the protection of states and the nation in other ways as well. These kinds of regulations often addressed the connection between militias and arms. For example, in Massachusetts, most able-bodied men between the ages of 18 and 50 were required to be available for service in the state militia. These men had to purchase and use their own arms for service, and the state would inspect and keep a record of the arms owned by each man. Several states had

It took time and effort to reload a colonial firearm.

similar militia laws, which framed arms ownership as a part of one's civic duty.

Other regulations in the late 1700s and early 1800s focused on public safety. Because gunpowder could be a dangerous and explosive substance, laws limited the amount that could be stored at businesses and homes. Some laws prohibited keeping loaded firearms in those places as well because of the potential for harm. Safety concerns also led to prohibitions of concealed weapons and the carrying of weapons in populated areas. According to an Ohio law from the 1800s, for instance, a person convicted of carrying a concealed weapon, including a pistol or knife, could be fined up to $200 or be imprisoned for up to one month. The wide range of arms regulations that existed before the Second Amendment as well as those that continued in the decades immediately after its passage demonstrate that arms liberties and arms control have gone hand in hand since the country's founding. Firearms were pivotal instruments in the Revolutionary War, and as such, they have served as important symbols of national values since.

DISCUSSION STARTERS

- Are arms necessary to protect against tyranny or to orchestrate successful revolutions against oppression? Can you think of any successful social or political movements that have been achieved without arms?

- How have guns evolved as symbols in American culture? What facts, legends, images, or figures come to mind when considering the links between gun culture and American culture?

- Why might states, both in the past and in the present, hold different views about gun rights?

CHAPTER 3

RACE AND ARMS RIGHTS POST-CIVIL WAR

Many freed slaves joined the Union army during
the Civil War.

As time passed and the country grew, changing
circumstances prompted changing views on firearms and
the laws that governed them. The events of the American
Civil War (1861–1865) in particular cast arms usage,
rights, and ownership in new contexts. Confederate soldiers
exercised their right to bear arms in an attack on the central
government. John Wilkes Booth assassinated President
Abraham Lincoln with a single-bullet pistol in 1865. The
emancipation of enslaved people highlighted unequal
applications of the right to bear arms across races.

The Thirteenth Amendment (1865) abolished slavery in 1865, and the Fourteenth Amendment established equal protection under the law three years later, but many black citizens still found themselves shut out from access to Second Amendment rights. Before the Civil War, there had been a long history of both racial inequality and gun rights. The post–Civil War era emphasized that even if rights seem to apply to all people, there are several factors, including race relations, that can interfere with how rights are interpreted and applied.

POSTWAR DISARMAMENT AND THE COLFAX MASSACRE

Prior to the Civil War, there were laws in place that prevented slaves and free blacks from bearing arms. These laws existed out of fear of slave revolts and minority uprisings, and they also reinforced the concept at the time that black people were not equal to white people and thus should not have access to the same rights. Furthermore, militia laws often prohibited black people and other racial minorities such as Native Americans from serving. After the Emancipation Proclamation, black enlistment in the Union army became more prevalent. Black people served in all kinds of roles, including in the artillery and infantry, where they used firearms alongside white soldiers. Despite the outcome of the Civil War and the enactment of new amendments, black citizens continued to face new laws aimed at prohibiting them from exercising many rights, including the right to bear arms.

However, the federal government sometimes provided firearms to black citizen militias. Such was the case in Colfax, Louisiana, where a scene of racial violence broke out on April 13, 1873. The incident unfolded after a controversial gubernatorial election. John McEnery, a former Confederate military commander, ran against William Pitt Kellogg, a Vermont-born politician.

DISARMAMENT PRACTICES

Immediately following the Civil War, many Southern states enacted Black Codes. These laws aimed at suppressing black rights, including the right to own firearms. Congress responded by passing the Freedmen's Bureau Act of 1866, part of which stated that several rights, including the right to bear arms, "shall be secured to and enjoyed by all the citizens without respect to race or color, or previous condition of slavery."[1] The Civil Rights Act of 1866 also guarded the right to arms regardless of race, and Congress passed the Fourteenth Amendment in 1868 to reinforce those acts and provide a strong statement in defense of equal rights.

Southern states reacted with laws that circumvented Congress's efforts to protect black rights. In Tennessee, for example, an 1870 law banned the sale of all handguns. The law made an exception for expensive models, which many whites already owned and which most black people could not afford. Furthermore, the law covered only new sales and thus disproportionately affected black citizens, who had only recently received federal protection to purchase firearms.

Among their many differences were the candidates' views on and support from racial groups. McEnery had backing from white supremacist organizations, while Kellogg supported black rights. The state's returning board, which was in charge of tallying election votes, declared McEnery the winner. However, Kellogg and his supporters challenged the results, arguing that the board had abused its power to include or exclude votes based on its own judgment. The board favored McEnery politically, and so Kellogg suspected bias in members' judgment. A federal judge later declared Kellogg the winner.

As a result of the dispute, Kellogg's administration encountered resistance when it tried to install local government officials in parts of the state. In Colfax, armed white men planned to overtake the courthouse rather than see new government officials take their posts. Armed black men stood in defense of the courthouse, but the white group had more firearms as well as a small cannon. The mob ordered the black men to lay down their weapons and surrender. The black defenders initially refused to do so, and the white group began its attack, quickly overpowering the black defenders and setting fire to the courthouse. The violence continued even as members of the black group fled for safety and tried to surrender. Estimates of the death toll vary, with some reaching

Families gather the dead and wounded after the
Colfax Massacre in 1873.

as high as 280, but most agree that more than 100 black

people were killed that day.[2]

THE COLFAX MASSACRE AND THE SUPREME COURT

The Colfax Massacre prompted one of the first legal cases on

the right to bear arms to reach the US Supreme Court. Though

dozens of white men were involved in the violence at Colfax,

only nine were prosecuted. Of those nine, only three were

convicted.[3] One of the convicted, William Cruikshank, appealed

DRED SCOTT V. SANDFORD

Though prior Supreme Court cases did not comment as directly on the Second Amendment as the *Cruikshank* case did, previous cases had considered the right of black individuals to keep and carry arms. In a well-known and often condemned case, *Dred Scott v. Sandford* (1857), the court identified access to arms as one of many reasons black people should not be allowed to become citizens. Acknowledging black people as citizens would give them access to the same liberties as whites, including the liberty to keep and carry arms. According to the ruling, affording black people that liberty would threaten the "peace and safety of the State."[4]

the case until it reached the Supreme Court. A key issue at stake was whether Cruikshank and other members of the white group had deprived the black men of their constitutional rights, including the right to bear arms. Until this point, the Supreme Court had made very little comment on the Second Amendment. With the Cruikshank case, however, the court had to interpret the amendment, explaining its meaning and application.

The Supreme Court ultimately decided in favor of Cruikshank in 1876, arguing that he had not violated the victims' Second Amendment rights. In his decision, Chief Justice Morrison Waite wrote that the right to bear arms "is not a right granted by the Constitution. Neither is it in any manner dependent upon that instrument for its existence. The second

amendment declares that it shall not be infringed; but this . . .
means no more than that it shall not be infringed by Congress."
Waite continued: "This is one of the amendments that has
no other effect than to restrict the powers of the national
government."[5] According to this interpretation, the Second
Amendment controls the actions of the federal government,
not those of states or private citizens. The federal government
had not interfered with the black men's right to bear arms in
Colfax. Private citizens had been responsible for the actions
there. Therefore, no violation of the Second Amendment
had occurred.

CONTEMPORARY VIEWS

In the view of some gun rights advocates, the years following
the Civil War demonstrate the dangers of gun control. White
supremacist groups such as the Ku Klux Klan began in part
as gun control organizations, and the effects of that control
proved tragic for black Americans. Forced disarmament of
black people by whites played out the violence colonists had
feared when the British attempted disarmament in the colonies
decades earlier. Moreover, according to this point of view, the
Cruikshank ruling exposed the need for stronger interpretations
of the Second Amendment. Interpretations of the Constitution
in the 1800s did not protect the Second Amendment rights

of all citizens in all circumstances. The case indicated that black citizens had to look to state and local governments for protection against disarmament. However, in the post–Civil War South, racism was often written into laws, and white supremacist groups such as the Ku Klux Klan were supported by local officials.

A Ku Klux Klan initiation near Atlanta, Georgia, in 1949

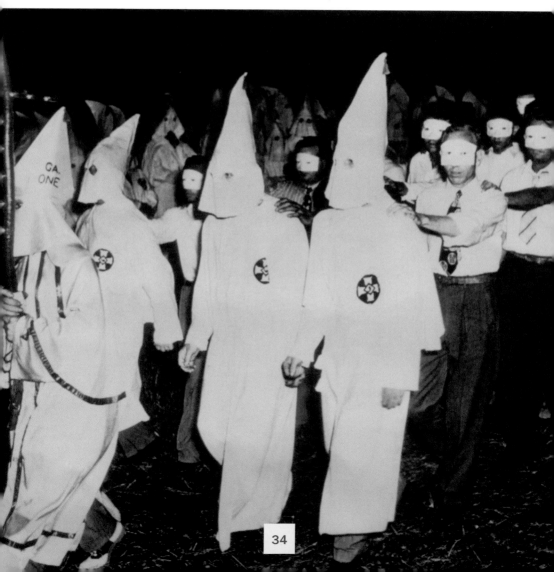

In other views, these events demonstrate the potential dangers in gun access. White supremacists used firearms, some obtained legally, as instruments of intimidation and force. In the face of violence, black people had little recourse. The *Cruikshank* case demonstrated how difficult it was to prosecute whites for violent gun crimes and for the disarmament of black citizens. When contemporary discussions of the right to bear arms focus on the years following the Civil War, both gun rights advocates and gun control advocates find evidence to support their positions. These discussions highlight how factors such as race have affected people's access to the right to bear arms.

DISCUSSION STARTERS

- Do the events of the Colfax Massacre support greater gun liberties for all or greater gun restrictions for all?

- How is racial gun violence different today than it was in the 1870s? Is there any connection between history and current trends?

- Adam Winkler, a law professor who studies the Constitution and gun rights, believes racism and race have impacted the development of gun laws. Do you agree? Why or why not?

CHAPTER 4

THE NATIONAL RIFLE ASSOCIATION

FREEDOM'S SAFEST PLACE

NRA

NRA members gather every year for a national convention.

The years following the Civil War were an important time for issues of race, gun rights, gun access, and interpretations of the Second Amendment. Those years also produced what is now one of the most influential groups among right-to-bear-arms proponents, the National Rifle Association (NRA). The NRA formed in response to the Civil War. During the war, Colonel William Church and General George Wingate, leaders in the Union military, observed poor marksman skills among their troops. In 1871, they founded the NRA to "promote and encourage rifle shooting on a scientific basis."[1]

Since its founding, the NRA has shifted focus from military preparedness, to general training and sportsmanship, to the rights advocacy and lobbying it is known for today.

PROMOTING MILITARY, EDUCATIONAL, AND SPORTS PROGRAMS

In its early years, the NRA was an educational organization that mostly focused on military preparedness and marksmanship. The NRA's founding members believed that by training marksmen they were providing an important national public service should there be another war. To achieve its goals, the group secured funds from the state of New York to buy its first property: a farm on Long Island named Creedmoor. In 1872, the NRA established a range at Creedmoor that it used for training and shooting competitions. However, Creedmoor closed in 1892 after some New York government officials argued that training in rifle skills was unnecessary during times of peace. The NRA then found new property in New Jersey.

Throughout the late 1800s and early 1900s, the NRA continued to host recreational events and shooting sports. Members also promoted rifle clubs at military academies and universities and were affiliated with youth programs to encourage proper training and safety. The NRA saw boosts in membership following US citizen involvement in wars

THEODORE ROOSEVELT

Theodore Roosevelt became president after the assassination of President William McKinley in 1901. Roosevelt was an avid hunter and conservationist throughout his life, and he served as a commander for a cavalry unit informally called the Rough Riders during the Spanish-American War. He supported gun use for recreation, self-defense, and military preparedness. Roosevelt signed a 1905 law that permitted the military to sell surplus firearms to NRA rifle clubs. Furthermore, he made a habit of writing congratulatory letters to the winners of the NRA's annual recreational shooting match. As president, he carried a gun on his person for protection. During a political campaign in 1912, Roosevelt was the subject of an assassination attempt. The bullet struck him in the chest and remained lodged there until his death in 1919.

Roosevelt had a keen appreciation for the workmanship involved in crafting a gun. He described one gun engraved with the presidential seal and his initials as "the prettiest gun I ever saw, and the mechanism as beautiful as that of a watch."[2] He had a similar respect for the skill of shooting. Roosevelt considered marksmanship, alongside camping and horsemanship, to be part of a naturalist lifestyle. These activities, he wrote, "teach observation, resourcefulness, self-reliance, [and] are within the reach of all who really care for the life of the woods, the fields, and the waters."[3]

Young Theodore Roosevelt poses with a rifle in an 1885 studio portrait.

such as the Spanish-American War (1898), World War I
(1914–1918), and World War II (1939–1945). After World
War II, the NRA noticed that some veterans had a stronger
interest in hunting than in shooting competitions. As a result,
the NRA adopted hunters into the population it served and
expanded its educational aims to include proper hunting safety
and etiquette.

MAKING A PLACE IN POLITICS

Today, the NRA is known for its powerful lobbying and its
interest in preventing legislation that would interfere with the
individual right to bear arms. The group's role in gun laws
evolved gradually in the 1900s. In 1905, the NRA supported
a law that would allow the military to sell extra firearms to
rifle clubs sponsored by the NRA. Through this measure,
NRA-affiliated programs obtained hundreds of thousands
of firearms from the federal government. In 1907, the NRA
acquired office space in Washington, DC. Then, in 1911, the
group unsuccessfully opposed a push for gun control laws
such as the Sullivan Act, which required people to get a permit
before buying or carrying a handgun. James Drain, the NRA
president at the time, argued that, though such regulations
were meant to keep criminals from getting weapons, they would
also prevent law-abiding citizens from obtaining firearms.

Even with those objections, the NRA compromised on some regulation efforts in the 1930s. The National Firearms Act proposed by President Franklin D. Roosevelt in 1934 was a notable federal effort to regulate firearms. The act came in response to gang violence in the 1920s that resulted in high-profile shoot-outs such as the infamous 1929 Saint Valentine's Day Massacre in Chicago. The NRA launched a letter-writing campaign to prevent restrictions its members believed were too limiting. In addition, it formed a legislative affairs division to monitor legal initiatives that might restrict firearms access and rights. However, the group did not object to all restrictions. For example, the group compromised on the 1934 act's strict control over the selling of machine guns and sawed-off shotguns. When the

A GOOD GUY WITH A GUN

In his objection to laws requiring permits to purchase or carry handguns, NRA president James Drain observed, "Such laws have the effect of arming the bad man and disarming the good one to the injury of the community."[4] This position still appears in contemporary debates over the right to bear arms. Some argue that criminals will always find illegal ways to obtain firearms. Therefore, federal oversight of gun ownership really only restricts law-abiding citizens, which can be harmful to individual and public safety. The NRA executive vice president in 2017, Wayne LaPierre, echoes this idea in his famous quotation, "The only way to stop a bad guy with a gun is with a good guy with a gun."[5]

US government passed another act, the Federal Firearms Act of 1938, the NRA compromised again to agree to bans that prevented the sale of guns to felons and fugitives and controlled the sale of guns across state lines without proper licensing.

CONSTITUTIONAL RIGHTS ACTIVISM

When asked about the constitutionality of the 1934 act, an NRA official noted, "I have not given it any study from that point of view."[6] No mention of the Constitution appeared on the inscription of the NRA's new Washington, DC, headquarters either. The building opened in 1958 to accommodate a bigger staff and a growing membership of hundreds of thousands of people. The inscription read, "FIREARMS SAFETY EDUCATION, MARKSMANSHIP TRAINING, SHOOTING FOR RECREATION."[7] The defense of constitutional rights did not become a significant goal of the NRA until later in the century.

The focus on defending constitutional rights began developing in response to events of the 1960s, when the NRA came to a crossroads in its identity and goals. The 1960s were a turbulent time for gun violence and gun rights in the country. Among those events was the assassination of President John F. Kennedy by Lee Harvey Oswald. Oswald had purchased the army rifle he used to kill Kennedy through an advertisement in

American Rifleman, a magazine published by the NRA. When ordering the weapon, Oswald used a fake name, A. Hidell, and it arrived through the mail. To close loopholes and curb gun violence, the federal government proposed the Gun Control Act of 1968. The president of the NRA at the time, General Franklin Orth, spoke of his support for the act in front of Congress: "We do not think that any sane American, who calls himself an American, can object to placing into this bill the instrument which killed the president of the United States."[8] He also wrote a piece explaining his support in the *American Rifleman*. In the article, he acknowledged that some of the act's provisions "appear unduly restrictive and unjustified in their application to law-abiding citizens, [but] the measure as a

UNITED STATES V. MILLER

The Supreme Court case *United States v. Miller* (1939) examined the constitutionality of the National Firearms Act of 1934. The court ruled it was legal for the federal government to regulate firearms and enforce registration of those arms. The court also connected the right to bear arms with service in the militia, arguing that sawed-off shotguns had no "reasonable relationship to the preservation or efficiency of a well regulated militia." Therefore, the court concluded, "we cannot say that the Second Amendment guarantees the right to keep and bear arms."[9] The ruling in this case came under debate in 2008 when the Supreme Court ruled that individuals had a right to possess arms for reasons other than service in a militia.

Wayne LaPierre has helped turn the National Rifle Association into a major political influence.

whole appears to be one that the sportsmen of America can live with."[10]

Some NRA members did not agree with Orth's position, nor did they support the direction in which gun control was headed based on such moves as the 1968 act. The disagreements came to a head at the NRA's annual meeting in 1977. Members who supported Orth believed the NRA should move away from politics and identify instead as a sportsmen's group, focusing on safety education, shooting competitions, hunting, and outdoor activities. Others thought the group needed to stand more firmly in politics, advocating against gun control legislation. At the meeting, members voted in favor of political advocacy for gun rights. That vote shifted the group's identity and cemented its place as a lobbying group. After that meeting, the NRA headquarters adopted a new motto: "The Right of the People to Keep and Bear Arms Shall Not Be Infringed."[11] The motto takes some wording from the Second Amendment, signaling that the NRA had begun to interpret the right to own and carry arms as a constitutional right for Americans.

The founding and development of the NRA emphasize that attitudes toward firearms have changed over time, both within the group and in the country in general. Today, behind Executive Vice President Wayne LaPierre, the NRA is one of the most outspoken lobbyist groups in the country. Because of its strong opinions, the

REVOLT AT CINCINNATI

Heading into the annual meeting of the NRA in 1977 in Cincinnati, Ohio, NRA leaders supported a group identity focused on sportsmanship and outdoor activities. But they faced an organized opposition. Those who disagreed gathered votes against the leadership by mobilizing members and using walkie-talkies to strategize secretly during the meeting. The movement worked, and meeting attendees voted out the organization's leaders and replaced them with people who supported the gun rights lobbying identity. While it was not a violent revolt, it was a planned overturn of sitting leadership.

#ALIYAH

6 YEAR'S OLD

#END GUN VIOLENCE

Born 10-11-05
Murdered 03-17-12

Six-year-old Caitlin Aguila holds a photo of her sister at a Coalition to Stop Gun Violence rally.

group often encounters opposition and controversy. Opponents argue that the NRA has misinterpreted the meaning of the Second Amendment and taken it out of context. For example, critics observe that the NRA does not adequately address the "well regulated militia" language of the Second Amendment. Furthermore, opponents claim that the NRA prioritizes the right to bear arms over other rights. The Coalition to Stop Gun Violence, for instance, asserts that "all Americans have a right to live in communities free from gun violence."[12] However, the NRA and its supporters consider themselves members of a civil rights organization with the persistent defense of the Second Amendment as its objective. Some argue that the organization is vital to protecting citizens' constitutional liberties.

DISCUSSION STARTERS

- Consider Wayne LaPierre's statement, "The only way to stop a bad guy with a gun is with a good guy with a gun." What are the merits of that claim? What are the fallacies?

- Today, the NRA faces criticism for its strong defense of gun rights even in the face of shooting tragedies. Is that criticism fair? What are reasonable ways the NRA could respond to such criticism?

- Do your perceptions of the NRA change when its history is taken into account?

CHAPTER 5

POLITICS AND ARMS RIGHTS IN THE 1960s

The 1960s were a tumultuous time in the United States, and firearm usage, rights, and regulations were woven into the upheaval. The assassination of Kennedy in 1963 was just one of many incidents in the 1960s that changed attitudes and laws on the right to bear arms. Other high-profile assassinations throughout the decade included the deaths of civil rights activists Medgar Evers in 1963, Malcolm X in 1965, and Martin Luther King Jr. in 1968. Senator Robert F. Kennedy—the president's brother—also was assassinated in 1968.

Lee Harvey Oswald poses with the rifle he would use to assassinate President John F. Kennedy.

Medgar Evers served as the state secretary for the NAACP.

These murders highlighted the threat of firearms in the wrong hands and raised questions about how easy it was for dangerous and unstable individuals to obtain guns. However, the tragedies also motivated people to seek out increased access to arms for the sake of protection. Factions of the civil rights movement emphasized the connection between gun rights, the defense of other rights, and personal safety during a period when racially motivated violence was a grave concern. Episodes of dangerous white supremacy coupled with bias among government agencies and law enforcement units led some black activists to see armament as a necessary step to defend life and rights. Thus, guns appeared as both a source of tragedy and a source of protection in the decade's civil rights and black advocacy movements.

BLACK ACTIVISTS AND ARMS ADVOCACY

Racial violence was a persistent fear in the 1960s. The shooting death of Evers on June 12, 1963, demonstrated the fear. Evers, who held a prominent position in the National Association for the Advancement of Colored People (NAACP), was shot in the driveway of his family's home in Jackson, Mississippi, late at night. The shooter, Byron De La Beckwith, was a white supremacist with ties to hate groups such as the White Citizen's Council and the Ku Klux Klan. Two murder trials failed to convict Beckwith, and evidence of law enforcement bias and jury tampering throughout the case added to concerns about safety and justice within the black community.

Black citizens had other reasons to distrust government officials and law enforcement when it came to matters of safety, self-defense, and preservation of rights. Instances of police brutality and arrests disproportionately affected black communities. In addition, urban uprisings over social and economic injustices often resulted in violent clashes between police and the black community. For example, in the summer of 1965, heated protests known as the Watts Riots broke out in South Los Angeles. The riot was incited by a controversial traffic stop involving a black driver and a white police officer.

PERSPECTIVES
CORETTA SCOTT KING

Coretta Scott King worked alongside her husband, Martin Luther King Jr., to promote a philosophy of nonviolence, and she continued that effort after his shooting death. On April 27, 1968, barely three weeks after her husband's assassination, King delivered a speech in which she condemned gun violence in American society and in US foreign policy. In that speech, King spoke of women's power to stand against gun violence and the social problems that lead to it: "The woman power of this nation can be the power which makes us whole and heals the rotten community, now so shattered by war and poverty and racism. . . . I believe that the women of this nation and the world are the best and last hope for a world of peace and brotherhood."[1]

King later founded the Martin Luther King Jr. Center for Nonviolent Social Change and served alongside Ethel Kennedy, Robert Kennedy's widow, as national cochair of the Coalition to Stop Gun Violence. Through both organizations, King advocated passionately to encourage understanding of the root causes behind gun violence, citing poverty and bigotry as two dominant factors.

In 1968, Coretta Scott King, *center*, speaks at a press conference about the death of her husband, Martin Luther King Jr.

That incident added another mark to a long list of grievances black citizens had with law enforcement and government officials. Citizens were frustrated by governmental neglect of their community. People experienced poor housing conditions, lack of opportunity and resources, substandard schools, and high unemployment. In response to the riots, the California government sent thousands of National Guard troops and implemented a curfew. The community had felt neglected before the riots, and the government response seemed to infringe upon residents' rights even further.

Prompted by politically charged murders, such as the assassination of Malcolm X, and other acts of racial violence, Bobby Seale and Huey Newton formed the Black Panther Party for Self-Defense in Oakland, California, in 1966. As the Black Panthers developed, they expressed their objectives in a ten-point platform. One of these points emphasized the right to bear arms in self-defense against government and police brutality: "The Second Amendment to the Constitution of the United States gives a right to bear arms. We therefore believe that all black people should arm themselves for self-defense."[2] Black Panther members studied gun laws, openly carried weapons, undertook action to arm other members, and patrolled their communities to protect their fellow citizens from violence. The Panthers' position on firearms has received

Bobby Seale, *left*, and Huey Newton were two of the founders of the Black Panther Party.

criticism as being extreme and dangerous, especially in comparison with other factions of the civil rights movement that had an emphasis on nonviolence, a philosophy promoted by Martin Luther King Jr. However, the Black Panthers believed extreme measures were necessary in the face of extreme threats to their rights.

GOVERNMENT RESPONSE WITH GUN CONTROL EFFORTS

California responded to black urban armament efforts with a push for strict gun control. The Mulford Act of 1967 sought to repeal a law that allowed people to carry loaded weapons in public as long as the weapons were readily visible. Black Panther members organized a protest at the state capitol, carrying loaded firearms with them, which was still legal since the bill had not passed yet. A skirmish broke out inside the building, and the Black Panthers were forced out even though they had not broken any laws. Outside, the Black Panthers read a statement, decrying lawmakers for "keeping the Black people disarmed and powerless."[3] Legislatures passed the bill, and the then governor Ronald Reagan signed it into law. The Black Panther Party did not disappear after that, but the act sought to delegitimize its efforts, criminalize its members' behavior, and undermine the group's community patrols.

Federal legislation—including the Gun Control Act of 1968—worked with state laws such as the Mulford Act to establish a broader trend of arms regulation. This was in response to the racial and political upheaval of the 1960s.

MIXED LEGACY OF THE BLACK PANTHERS

The Mulford Act undercut one of the Black Panthers' aims, but rather than destroying the group, the act roused its membership and attracted national attention to the party. At various points in its history, the Black Panthers have held different reputations: community service organizers, outspoken black power advocates, communist sympathizers, and radical, militant separatists. The group finally dissolved in the early 1980s due to a combination of many factors, including internal disagreement over future goals, efforts of the US government to limit its activity, and a lack of funding. Regarding the party's legacy and its impact on the right to bear arms, historian Waldo Martin and sociologist Joshua Bloom observe that the Black Panthers "reinvented the politics of armed self-defense" by promoting arms as tools of black self-determination and "resistance to the state."[4]

CRIMINAL ARMS

The shooting tragedies in the 1960s raised questions about how accessible guns were to individuals with a history of unstable or criminal behavior. Prior to purchasing his weapon, Lee Harvey Oswald had spent a week in a Soviet hospital after a suicide attempt. Other signs of his instability included an arrest for disturbance of the peace, the revocation of his honorable discharge from the US military, and a history of political extremism.

James Earl Ray, who shot Martin Luther King Jr., was a fugitive who had escaped from a Missouri prison. Ray had spent more than 13 years in prison for holdups and burglaries.

These tragedies also pointed to the issue of people obtaining weapons through questionable channels or procuring weapons that were already illegal. Sirhan Sirhan, who killed Robert Kennedy, was a political extremist who wrote obsessively about killing the senator as retribution for US policies in Israel. He used a gun his brother had purchased informally from a teenager. One of the men who killed Malcolm X used a sawed-off shotgun, which had been illegal since 1934.

These regulations extended some national oversight of arms usage, possession, and transfer. For example, one of the provisions of the 1968 act changed the name of the Alcohol and Tobacco Tax Division to the Bureau of Alcohol, Tobacco and Firearms (ATF). According to its website, the ATF is in charge of licensing "the sale, possession, and transportation of firearms, ammunition, and explosives" between states "to curb the illegal use of firearms and enforce the Federal firearms laws."[5]

These new regulations had an

unexpected effect. High-profile political assassinations of the 1960s helped thrust gun control conversations onto the national stage, and race, civil rights, and racial violence consistently served as an important backdrop in those conversations and in new legislation. Many of the laws targeted arms activity in urban black communities and among black power advocates. However, according to constitutional law professor Adam Winkler, the 1960s gun regulations created "a backlash that became the modern gun rights movement—a movement that, ironically, is largely white, rural, and politically conservative."[6] That backlash was evident in the NRA's Cincinnati revolt of 1977, and it continued to grow as gun regulation stiffened toward the end of the 1900s.

DISCUSSION STARTERS

- How do the Black Panthers' experiences compare with those of the black citizens who endured the Colfax Massacre?

- Are there parallels between the colonists' concerns about government and disarmament and civil rights activists' concerns about government and disarmament? Are there differences?

- In what ways are the Black Panther Party and the NRA similar? In what ways are they different?

CHAPTER 6

THE BRADY CAMPAIGN

Former White House press secretary James Brady, *right*, discusses gun control with President Bill Clinton in 1993.

Even as arms regulation stiffened following the 1960s, dramatic shooting events persisted into the following decades. One such event occurred on March 30, 1981, when an assassination attempt was made on President Ronald Reagan. Nobody was killed the day of the attack, but James Brady, the president's press secretary, sustained a gunshot to the head that paralyzed him for the rest of his life. He died on August 4, 2014, and the medical examiner ruled his death a homicide because it was directly related to the injuries

John Hinckley Jr., *left*, after a court appearance in 1984

he suffered during the shooting. The would-be assassin, John Hinckley Jr., was found not guilty by reason of insanity.

Before his death, Brady and his wife, Sarah, became vocal members of the gun control movement. In the mid-1980s, the Bradys joined Handgun Control Inc. (HCI). The gun control advocacy group had formed in the 1960s in response to the many high-profile shootings at the time. The group later changed its name to become the Brady Campaign to Prevent Gun Violence because of the Bradys' pivotal role in the organization. Since the 1980s and 1990s, the Brady Campaign has taken on a broad gun control mission to drastically reduce the number of gun fatalities in the United States. Though the Brady Campaign began after a high-profile shooting incident, much of its focus is now on less dramatic shooting incidents that occur in cities and homes every day—incidents of street violence, domestic violence, accidents, and suicides. While not as eye-catching as assassinations and public shootings, these incidents account for the majority of gun-related injuries and deaths in the country. The Brady Campaign positions the right to bear arms alongside the rights that arms may potentially infringe.

THE BRADY ACT AND LEGAL INITIATIVES

For many years, Sarah Brady's primary effort was advocating for the Brady Handgun Violence Prevention Act to pass into law. Legislation for

JOHN HINCKLEY JR.

Among John Hinckley's mental problems was an obsession with the actress Jodie Foster, which developed after he saw her in the movie *Taxi Driver*. In order to attract Foster's attention, Hinckley tried to emulate the actions of the movie's main character, Travis Bickle. Those actions included amassing weapons and stalking a presidential candidate. After being found not guilty by reason of insanity, Hinckley was committed to a mental health hospital to treat psychosis and depression. In 2016, doctors at the hospital determined Hinckley's illnesses were in remission and that he did not pose a danger to himself or others. As a result of that determination, Hinckley was released from the mental hospital. Hinckley's right to bear arms has not been restored, however. As a condition of his release, Hinckley cannot possess weapons, but he does have other liberties, such as access to a driver's license.

the Brady Act first appeared before lawmakers in 1988, but it took seven years of advocacy for the legislation to become law. The law passed on November 30, 1993, and new gun control guidelines became effective in 1994. Amending the Gun Control Act of 1968, the Brady Act enforced background check requirements in the 32 states that did not yet have strong measures in place. The other 18 states and Washington, DC, already had measures in effect that were comparable to those enforced in the Brady Act. As the text of the law says, these background checks focused on preventing gun sales to people with "felony convictions, histories of mental illness, or other disqualifying characteristics."[1] In those 32 states, the act also required a five-day waiting period before "a licensed importer, manufacturer, or dealer" could "sell, deliver, or transfer a handgun to an unlicensed individual."[2]

Since the passage of the Brady Act, the Brady Campaign has continued to advocate for public policy and legal action to keep guns out of the hands of those it describes as having "criminal or harmful intent."[3] The group aims to do so by closing gun sale loopholes such as straw purchases, private sales, and Internet sales. Private sales and Internet sales also can result in problems because those sales often have a no-questions-asked, no-background-check policy. The Brady Campaign supports legislation to reduce these loopholes.

Furthermore, to counteract the problem of stolen weapons, the group encourages implementing technology that will prevent a gun from firing for anyone except the gun's legal owner. With these initiatives, the Brady Campaign hopes to curb arms exchanges that happen without background checks and the violence that stems from them.

GUN VIOLENCE VICTIMS ON THE STREET AND IN THE HOME

Guns used in urban street crimes, which the Brady Campaign argues are too easily obtainable, create a web of victims in disadvantaged areas. In surveys reviewed by the National Institute of Justice, offenders in a wide range of crimes reported that most of the guns they acquired came through illicit channels.

Furthermore, "more than half the arrestees say it is easy to obtain guns illegally."[4] These arms often play a role in urban, drug-related, and gang-related violence. Such gun usage arises from and contributes

STRAW PURCHASES

The Brady Campaign refers to vendors who knowingly fulfill straw purchases as "bad apples," and the group points out that a small number of bad apples are responsible for circulating many of the guns used in crimes. In fact, the campaign reports that just 5 percent of dealers—those they call the bad apples—supply about 90 percent of guns used in crimes. The Brady Campaign's efforts target these dealers more than they do law-abiding sellers.[5]

to a cycle of violence and hopelessness in depressed communities. In these communities, the people who perpetrate gun violence are often the people who are victimized by it, though bystanders may be victimized as well. Overwhelmingly, the people locked in these cycles are poor, young, black males who have grown up in homes and social environments that put them at risk.

Guns obtained illegally and used in urban street crimes account for only part of the problem. As the Brady Campaign notes, legally purchased and owned guns are responsible for most US gun injuries and deaths, many of which occur in suburban settings. Of those deaths, most are suicides, including suicides in which a young victim uses a gun legally owned by a parent or adult acquaintance. Other deaths are due to accidents, including those involving children who find and discharge an adult's gun while playing or exploring. Gun usage in cases of domestic violence is a grave concern as well. Overall, the Brady Campaign reports that firearms, both legally and illegally obtained, account for 33,880 deaths and 81,114 injuries per year in the United States.[6]

A PUBLIC HEALTH CRISIS

By drawing attention to the problems in both urban and suburban settings, involving arms obtained both legally and illegally, the Brady Campaign illustrates that gun violence is a complex, nationwide problem. As a result, the problem requires a nationwide effort to reach a solution. In advocating for a solution, the Brady Campaign now frames the gun violence problem as a public health issue that interferes with people's rights to life, happiness, safety, and freedom. The group compares troublesome gun usage to commonly accepted dangers such as drunk driving and secondhand smoke inhalation. As such, the

DOMESTIC VIOLENCE

Domestic violence affects both men and women, though women are more likely than men to become victims of abuse. According to the National Coalition against Domestic Violence, that abuse is 500 percent more likely to turn fatal if a gun is present.[7] To protect women, public health researchers suggest that communities and medical professionals take action to warn abused women of the possibility of gun violence. These warnings can help women devise plans to escape abusive partners without suffering further violence.

Laws that prohibit people with a history of domestic violence from passing background checks can help protect victims. Advocacy groups note that background checks have resulted in hundreds of thousands of denials to people with domestic abuse histories.[8] However, these groups note that there is more work to be done to close safety gaps. For instance, some laws prevent domestic abusers from purchasing new guns but do not require them to give up arms they already own. In another example, some laws protect people whose spouses have a history of domestic abuse, but the laws don't apply if the attacker and victim aren't married.

Brady Campaign argues the United States should approach gun usage with the same kind of public awareness efforts and education programs that successfully helped to stigmatize drunk driving and smoking. By doing so, the campaign aims to change attitudes, actions, behaviors, and social norms among lawful gun owners and society in general.

With the combination of legislative initiatives and public outreach programs, the Brady Campaign aims to help decrease all forms of gun casualties. While critics of the Brady Campaign claim that the group uses alarmist tactics to threaten an essential right to arms, the Brady Campaign argues that advocates must defend the other rights of vulnerable populations, such as health, safety, security, and happiness. For the Brady Campaign, the right to bear arms is not more important than those rights.

DISCUSSION STARTERS

- Do the NRA and the Brady Campaign have any common ground on the right to bear arms?

- Should criminals be allowed to regain their gun rights after serving their sentences? Or is it a right that should be permanently revoked?

- The Brady Campaign compares gun violence to secondhand smoking or drunk driving. Is that a fair or useful comparison?

Gun rights advocates argue that the right to bear arms is inalienable and that infringing on that right is a threat to freedom.

CHAPTER 7

INDIVIDUAL RIGHTS AND SELF-DEFENSE

Dick Anthony Heller speaks outside the Supreme Court in 2008.

In the early 2000s, Dick Anthony Heller worked as a security guard at the Federal Judicial Center, where he had the authority to carry a handgun while on duty. Heller wanted to keep a handgun at his home as well. To keep the gun in his home legally, he had to apply to register it. However, his application was denied because of gun control laws established in Washington, DC, during the 1970s in an attempt to decrease violence in the area. Those laws included a ban preventing the new registration of handguns, prohibitions against carrying handguns, and a safe-storage requirement, which meant that all firearms had to be kept unloaded, disassembled, or trigger locked when stored in homes. Heller believed these laws undermined personal safety and self-defense because they prevented people from having ready access to guns in their homes in case of an emergency. He also believed the laws violated his constitutional rights.

Heller approached the NRA about taking his case, but the NRA declined. It worried that, should the case fail, it would draw negative attention to gun rights efforts as well as make it harder to preserve gun rights. Heller found attorneys willing to take the case at two libertarian organizations, the Institute for Justice and the Cato Institute. In 2008, the case went all the way to the Supreme Court, where five justices supported Heller's position and four opposed it. *District of Columbia v. Heller* was a landmark case because it defined the Second Amendment as an individual right preserved by the Constitution rather than as a collective right linked to service in a militia. The case has influenced contemporary understandings of and debates about the right to bear arms for personal self-defense.

BACKGROUND AND DECISION IN THE CASE

Before the *Heller* case, there had been very few Supreme Court cases examining the Second Amendment. One of those was the *Cruikshank* case arising from the events of the Colfax Massacre. Another was *United States v. Miller*. In *Miller*, the Supreme Court considered the 1934 act that banned sawed-off shotguns. The Court decided the ban could remain in place because those shotguns were not connected to the kinds of weapons used in a state militia. The *Heller* case reopened discussion about the Second Amendment, the right to bear arms, and the connection to state militias. Before *Heller*, most legal interpretations

DISSENT, LIMITATIONS OF *HELLER*

In his dissenting opinion in *Heller*, Justice John Paul Stevens asserts, "Until today, it has been understood that legislatures may regulate the civilian use and misuse of firearms so long as they do not interfere with the preservation of a well-regulated militia."[1] Stevens notes that the decision "upsets" the established, historical definition of the amendment. Furthermore, he argues that the new interpretation will give future courts a difficult task: determining when a private citizen is using a weapon lawfully and when a private citizen is using a weapon unlawfully.

The *Heller* decision supports the use of firearms by private citizens for "traditionally lawful purposes." However, Justice Scalia qualifies, "Like most rights, the Second Amendment right is not unlimited." The *Heller* decision defends restrictions on firearm ownership by felons and the mentally ill. It also supports laws that would prevent carrying arms in "sensitive places," including schools and government buildings, and allows for laws that prohibit firearms that are especially unusual or dangerous.[2]

considered the amendment as expressing a collective right: states, which represented a collective group of people, had a right to maintain an armed and well-regulated militia. Since the Second Amendment did not mention the link between an individual citizen and gun ownership, that right did not seem to be specifically granted in the Constitution.

Heller changed the interpretation. In a 5–4 decision, the Supreme Court justices affirmed Heller's position about arms and his right to them. Expressing the opinion of the majority, Justice Antonin Scalia wrote that "the Second Amendment protects an individual right to possess firearms. . . . The city's total ban on handguns, as well as its requirement that firearms in the home be kept nonfunctional even when necessary for

US Supreme Court Justice Antonin Scalia

self-defense, violated that right."[3] This decision provided a new legal perspective on the right to bear arms, arguing that it was an individual, constitutional right for all Americans, similar to the right to free speech. The decision notes that people have the right to bear arms for reasons other than those related to service in a state militia, such as for self-defense.

WHEN SELF-DEFENSE GOES RIGHT AND WHEN SELF-DEFENSE GOES WRONG

The *Heller* case has stirred broader debates about the extent of arms rights as they apply to self-defense. Proponents of *Heller* and self-defense gun laws point to the many instances in which victims have used firearms to ward off attackers. In Ohio, for example, people are allowed to carry concealed handguns for self-defense if they meet certain criteria, including proof of a background check free of felonies, mental illnesses, and restraining orders. The Buckeye Firearms Association keeps a record of documented stories involving handguns and successful self-defense. Some examples include a pizza-shop worker who defended himself and the store against a robber armed with a sawed-off shotgun, a woman who scared off a would-be rapist, and a couple who stopped a man from beating his girlfriend in front of her children by ordering him to the ground and holding him at gunpoint until police arrived.

Others are more critical of the *Heller* ruling and laws that protect gun use for self-defense. Opponents offer a range of examples to support their position. Often these examples

TRAYVON MARTIN

The Trayvon Martin case received national attention because it demonstrated the ambiguity of self-defense laws while raising speculation about racial profiling. Zimmerman, a 28-year-old white Hispanic volunteer community watchman, called 911 to report Martin, a black teenager, as a suspicious individual. Zimmerman claimed he was concerned about previous burglaries in his community. When he told the 911 operator that he was following Martin, the operator replied, "We don't need you to do that."[4] Meanwhile, Martin, who was walking home after buying snacks at a convenience store, called his girlfriend to tell her a man in a car was watching him.

A fight broke out. Zimmerman produced and fired his gun, which he had a permit to carry. Zimmerman suffered a broken nose and abrasions to his head. Martin was killed. A criminal justice expert at the Cato Institute argued that Florida's self-defense laws did not apply to Zimmerman because Martin committed no crime in Zimmerman's presence, nor was he initially aggressive. However, the jurors' inability to convict Zimmerman of murder or manslaughter demonstrates the differing understandings of those laws.

emphasize shootings in which someone is mistaken for an intruder. For instance, a man in North Carolina shot and killed his wife as she arrived home from her night shift job earlier than usual. A firefighter in Maryland died after he was shot while attempting to perform a wellness check on an ill man. The man's brother had requested the check, but the firefighter and his partners were mistaken for intruders. Other examples highlight the potential for misconstructions and even aggressive use of self-defense laws. In a now infamous

WE ARE ALL TRAYVON MARTIN

People throughout the country protested racial profiling after the
death of Trayvon Martin.

Florida case, George Zimmerman claimed self-defense when
he shot and killed Trayvon Martin, an unarmed 17-year-old.
Though accounts suggest violence could have been avoided,
the jury found Zimmerman not guilty of murder or manslaughter
because of Florida's self-defense laws.

At both extremes of the right to bear arms debate, people
fear slippery slopes. Strong gun rights advocates fear that
any regulation could snowball into complete disarmament.
Strong gun control advocates fear that lack of regulation could
descend into unchecked use of all kinds of arms by all kinds
of people. In his opinion for the court, Justice Scalia wrote
that *Heller* did not negate laws restricting dangerous people
from legally accessing dangerous weapons. However, Justice
John Paul Stevens wrote about the potential for a complicated

ELENA KAGAN

Elena Kagan received confirmation to the Supreme Court after the *Heller* ruling. Her position on gun rights and gun control was a point of debate during her confirmation process. Lawmakers and the general public pressed for information about her views on the Second Amendment, asking, "Well, have you ever held a gun?"[5] Kagan admitted that she had little experience with guns, but she promised to ask Justice Antonin Scalia to take her hunting if she were to be confirmed.

Both Scalia and Kagan followed through on the promise. The two began bird shooting a few times a year and then moved up to big game hunting. In 2013, Kagan said, "We actually went out to Wyoming this past fall to shoot deer and antelope, and we did. . . . I shot myself a deer."[6] Kagan viewed the hunting trips as a way to bond and learn about each other's differences. The recent attention paid to justices' legislative and personal experience with the right to bear arms places the Second Amendment alongside other hot-button rights issues such as abortion and gay marriage.

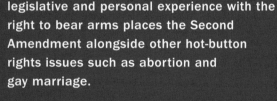

US Supreme Court Justice Elena Kagan

slippery slope. The *Heller* decision allows people to keep handguns in their homes for self-defense. However, Justice Stevens notes, "The need to defend oneself may suddenly arise in a host of locations outside the home, [and so] I fear that the District's policy choice may well be just the first of an unknown number of dominoes to be knocked off the table."[7] In the years following the *Heller* decision and in light of self-defense successes and self-defense mistakes, debates have continued. On one hand, the case is viewed as an example of sensible gun compromise and responsible usage. On the other, it is viewed as a decision that allows for legal gun usage in potentially erroneous or aggressive ways.

DISCUSSION STARTERS

- Compare the Supreme Court views of the right to bear arms expressed in the *Heller* case with those expressed earlier in the 1875 *Cruikshank* case. What has changed? What has not changed? Do you agree with one viewpoint more than the other? Why?

- Should there be limitations on the right to bear arms? If so, should those limits apply to types of weapons, types of people, reasons for gun ownership, and/or places where guns can be carried?

- How is the right to bear arms similar to or different from other rights the Constitution protects, such as freedom of speech, freedom of religion, or the right to remain silent?

CHAPTER 8

MASS SHOOTINGS AND MENTAL HEALTH

In 2007, Seung-Hui Cho killed 32 people on the campus of Virginia Polytechnic Institute. In 2011, Jared Loughner killed six people in a shopping center parking lot where Congresswoman Gabrielle Giffords was meeting with constituents. In 2012, Adam Lanza killed 20 first graders and six educators at Sandy Hook elementary school. Earlier that same year, James Holmes had opened fire at a midnight showing of a Batman movie and killed 12 people. In 2015, Dylann Roof killed nine congregants at Emanuel African Methodist Episcopal Church after a prayer meeting. In 2016,

A relative of a slain Virginia Tech student receives a posthumous degree for her brother one month after the shooting.

Omar Mateen killed 49 people in a shooting at an Orlando, Florida, nightclub. In 2017, Stephen Paddock killed 58 people when he fired on a crowd of concertgoers in Las Vegas, Nevada. The death toll for this shooting made it the worst of the mass public shootings in the United States in recent decades. These are just a few examples. In the 40 years between 1966 and 2006, more than 100 Americans committed mass shootings.[1] From 2000 to 2013, there were more than four mass shootings in the United States per year.[2]

Even so, these mass shooting events account for a small fraction of

HISTORY OF MASS SHOOTINGS

Mass shootings are not a new occurrence in the United States. In 1891, an assailant opened fire on a school assembly in Mississippi. There were no deaths in the incident, but 14 people suffered injuries, some serious.[3] In 1949, Howard Unruh, a World War II veteran later diagnosed as a paranoid schizophrenic, killed 13 people in his neighborhood of East Camden, New Jersey.[4] Researchers often identify a shooting at the University of Texas in 1966 as a precursor to patterns seen in many modern shootings. Charles Whitman, a 25-year-old former marine, stockpiled powerful firearms equipment, climbed a 27-story clock tower, and began firing at people in the plaza below. He killed 17 people as well as his mother and wife.[5] Prior to the attack, he had visited the university's psychological services, where he described violent shooting fantasies. After the attack, an autopsy revealed a brain tumor that may have impacted his behavior.

Charles Whitman used an arsenal of weapons to shoot at people from a tower on the University of Texas campus in 1966.

gun deaths, far fewer than the number of gun deaths linked to individual homicides, suicides, and accidents that take place every day. They often attract more attention because they are concentrated, overwhelming, and traumatic. They intrude into places where gun violence normally does not occur—schools, places of worship, entertainment venues, and workplaces. Such tragedies inevitably provoke examination of what led to them and what can be done to prevent mass shootings in the future. In examinations, a common current area of focus is mental health.

COURT CASES AND MENTAL HEALTH

Several perpetrators of recent mass shootings have suffered from mental illness. As a child, Cho had been diagnosed with a social anxiety disorder and major depression. At Virginia Tech, he produced violent writings, disrupted classes to the point where other students stopped attending, stalked female students, harassed students in their dorm rooms, threatened suicide, and was held for a brief time for psychiatric evaluation. Lanza also had been diagnosed with mental illness as a child. Lanza also was obsessive-compulsive; phobic of touch; hypersensitive to light, sound, and smells; paranoid; severely socially impaired; and dangerously underweight. Lanza's father suspected additional, severe illness, including schizophrenia, had gone undiagnosed. Both Cho and Lanza killed themselves as police closed in on the scenes of their mass shootings.

Other shooters survived, but their court cases show the legal complications of addressing mental illness and mass shooting crimes. Holmes had visited his university's mental health services, where he shared violent, homicidal thoughts with a therapist. During his trial, medical experts commented on Holmes's struggle with schizophrenia, and though Holmes was found guilty of charges related to the shooting, jurors declined to sentence him to death because of his mental illness. Loughner suffered such severe mental illness that he initially was deemed unfit to stand trial. Loughner was not formally diagnosed with schizophrenia until after his shooting arrest, but he had demonstrated a strong pattern of instability, risky behavior, and interest in violence throughout his teens and

Jared Loughner killed six people and wounded several more at an event held by US representative Gabrielle Giffords in Tucson, Arizona.

twenties. These factors led to several run-ins with security while he was a student, culminating in his suspension from Pima Community College. The college stipulated that he could not return until he received a mental health evaluation.

LEGAL REGULATIONS AND MENTAL ILLNESS

The Gun Control Act of 1968 and many state and local regulations since then have included sections that deny gun ownership to people who are mentally ill or who have been committed to a mental health institution. Under the law, an authority must have determined that the individual is a threat to himself or herself or to others. Despite existing laws, continuing links between mass shooters and mental illness have led to calls for stricter regulations. Of the four shooters discussed, all but Lanza purchased their firearms legally. Lanza got his weapons from a store of firearms that his mother bought and kept legally in the family home. Purchases by Cho, Holmes, and Loughner suggest gaps and ambiguities in the laws. Cho, for example,

GUNS IN SENSITIVE PLACES

Some public places, such as schools and government buildings, are considered sensitive places. In these places, there are often stricter regulations on the concealed and open carrying of weapons, including the need to obtain special licenses. Despite being places where arms are most strictly controlled, these are also places where mass shooting violence concentrates. As a result, some argue for increased open and concealed carry in sensitive places as a deterrent to potential gun violence. Others claim that expanded open and concealed carry in sensitive places would lead to more violence and less security.

purchased his gun even after a judge filled out paperwork deeming him to be mentally ill, a danger to himself, and in need of psychiatric care. The judge argued that he could not restrict Cho's right to bear arms because Cho had not been ordered into a mental health hospital. Some argue the vague wording that allowed the judge's interpretation needs to be clearer.

Stricter regulations for those with mental illness are among the gun control efforts with the most popular support. A national public opinion survey conducted by the New England Journal of Medicine in January 2013 found that "gun policies with the highest support included those related to persons with mental illness."[6] Among the policies receiving support was one that permitted a lifetime ban on arms access for people who had lost the right to bear arms for a mental health reason. That means that a person who has received treatment for and recovered from mental illness would never see his or her gun rights restored. One popular initiative includes increased funding to maintain accurate reporting and current databases for background checks. Other initiatives include more consistency in the application of laws and clearer wording in laws to close gaps.

Dylann Roof was arrested after shooting and killing nine people at a church in Charleston, South Carolina.

CRITIQUING THE MENTAL ILLNESS CONNECTION

Many social researchers and health-care professionals warn against drawing a connection between mass shootings and mental illness. Doing so can create an inaccurate perception of mental illness's relationship to violence. Data from 2001 to 2010 showed mentally ill individuals perpetrated less than 5 percent of gun homicides.[7] The vast majority of people who suffer from mental illness do not commit violent crimes, let alone mass shootings. Thus, these false perceptions feed into a harmful stigma that labels people with mental illness as criminals. In reality, people with mental illness are more likely to suffer violence at the hands of others than they are to perpetrate violence themselves.

Critics argue that the focus on mental health occurs after mass shootings because it creates a sense that society can protect itself against horrific tragedies. But, say these critics, the focus on mental illness is misplaced. Rather, these studies should focus on the many complex factors intersecting in mass shooting events. Other factors that need to be considered are the shooters' histories with substance abuse, economic stress, and rocky personal relationships. In addition, some mass shooters have shared their own motives for their crimes.

MASCULINITY AND MASS SHOOTINGS

Perpetrators of mass shootings tend to be men in their twenties. Douglas Kellner calls this phenomenon a "crisis of masculinity."[8] To understand and perhaps prevent mass shootings, Kellner argues, there must be further study of the link between social constructions of masculinity in the United States and instances of mass shootings. Though mass shooters are very often male, there have been mass shootings perpetrated by women. For example, in 2006, Jennifer San Marco killed her neighbor and six people at the mail facility where she had once worked.[9] She then committed suicide. Before the shooting, San Marco had demonstrated erratic behavior and experienced paranoid delusions suggestive of mental illness.

White supremacy motivated Dylann Roof's mass shooting, and ISIS-related terrorism motivated Omar Mateen's killings. Some have speculated about undiagnosed mental illness in both Roof and Mateen at the time of their crimes, but there were also broader webs of factors behind their violence. Mental illness alone, advocates claim, cannot explain their actions or those of other mass shooters.

Mass shootings provoke strong reactions as society searches for the reasons and some lead calls for action. In response to the mass shootings of this century, attention has focused strongly on mental illness. As a result, many people favor stricter and clearer prohibitions on gun rights for the mentally ill. However, discussion of those restrictions also prompts questions about discrimination and infringement of individual rights. Individuals with mental health conditions could find their rights at risk if it becomes too difficult to obtain a weapon. Some also argue that laws must allow those who have recovered from mental health problems to regain their right to arms. Others believe it is okay to infringe on individual liberties if the gun restrictions advance public safety.

DISCUSSION STARTERS

- Should individuals have to pass a physical or mental evaluation to qualify for gun ownership?

- Are gun regulations that restrict ownership among people diagnosed with mental illness a form of discrimination?

- Would the presence of guns make schools safer places? If so, who should be allowed to carry guns? Consider whether guards, resource officers, teachers, administrators, and college students should be allowed or even required to carry guns.

CHAPTER 9

THE FUTURE OF THE RIGHT TO BEAR ARMS

Gun ownership is a complex issue with a spectrum of opinions existing on both sides.

Lily Raff McCaulou grew up in the metro area of Washington, DC, far removed from the gun culture more familiar in rural areas of the country. When McCaulou moved to Oregon, she found herself drawn to that culture. She learned to hunt and fish, calling the experiences "life-affirming," "a chance to participate in an ecosystem," and a "stake in the health of wildlife populations."[1] McCaulou considers herself to be progun, but she emphasizes that her version of being progun may differ from someone else's. "There's a whole spectrum of gun owners," she says, "and I think one of the problems that we have as a country is that there is a very, very narrow view of the gun owner that has a voice."[2] The same observation also could be applied to those who do not own guns.

Splitting positions on the right to bear arms into two categories—progun or anti-gun—and giving those categories strict definitions oversimplifies the long, complex history of the right to bear arms in the United States. Individual opinions run along a wide spectrum, and concerns about the Second Amendment continue. The Black Lives Matter movement echoes the concerns among black citizens that the Second Amendment doesn't seem to apply to them. Legal policy has varied too, changing over time. Often legal policy has differed from state to state and among local, state, and federal governments. To this point, recent events indicate that the right to bear arms will continue

THE BLACK LIVES MATTER MOVEMENT

The Black Lives Matter movement calls attention to continued societal racism in the United States, focusing on violence against black people and the vilification of black victims. Black Lives Matter began in 2013 after George Zimmerman was acquitted in the shooting death of Trayvon Martin. It has since emphasized police shootings of black civilians. The movement recalls the outrage over racially motivated violence in the years following the Civil War and again in the 1960s. It emphasizes that racially charged violence and systemic oppression of African Americans continues today.

Black Lives Matter protests have spread to the United Kingdom, where these demonstrators marched in 2016.

to raise heated debate and draw close scrutiny in the years to come.

VIEWS EVOLVE

William Vizzard, a professor emeritus of criminal justice, observes that public opinions, laws, and judicial interpretations of the Second Amendment have changed throughout history, with some of the most radical changes coming in the last few decades. It is reasonable to think that public opinions, laws, and judicial interpretations will continue evolving.

In the past, legislation has responded to changes in national demographics and geographic expansion. It's also responded to social movements, political events, instances of violence, technological advancements in firearms, and technological changes impacting gun sales (such as the onset of Internet sales).

Weapons technology may pose some of the biggest questions regarding the right to bear arms in the future. In the *Heller* decision, Justice Antonin Scalia argued that the Second Amendment extends to "all instruments that constitute bearable arms, even those that were not in existence at the time of the founding."[3] At the same time, *Heller* supports earlier Supreme Court decisions that restrict individuals from carrying "dangerous and unusual weapons."[4]

Firearms have changed since the 1700s. Arms available in contemporary society are more accurate and can discharge more ammunition in a shorter period of time. Government regulation has addressed some technological changes as they have arisen. For example, fully automatic weapons are generally banned for individual civilian use in the United States. It might become more complicated to determine what qualifies as a "bearable" firearm and what qualifies as a "dangerous and unusual" weapon in the future.

The right to bear arms is also a deeply personal matter for many. People may have long-standing family traditions rooted in gun culture, they may embrace a hunting lifestyle, or they may enjoy a hobby or even a career of sport shooting. People may have firsthand connections to arms through military service. Others may have lost a loved one to gun violence or suicide. Some have successfully defended themselves with a gun. Furthermore, attitudes on the right to bear arms may be tied up with a person's religious

GUN LAWS AROUND THE WORLD

The constitutional right to bear arms in the United States differs from the contemporary approach to gun ownership in many other democracies. In Japan, for example, the law prohibits gun ownership except in limited circumstances. Private citizens may own arms only for competitions, hunting, research, or for particular jobs. People who want a gun for one of those purposes must go through an extensive application process. It includes classes, a shooting test, a written test, medical records proving physical and mental health, and a police investigation of the person's background and family to ensure there are no dangerous motives. Once a Japanese citizen owns a gun, he or she must follow strict storage requirements and ammunition regulations.

The United Kingdom also is known for its tight gun laws, enacted in the last 30 years in response to violent incidents. British citizens now must have a specific reason to own a firearm beyond simple self-defense, and they must have direct permission from governmental authorities.

Sport shooting has been part of the Olympic Games for more than a century.

beliefs, economic status, educational experience, job, location, race, gender, and many other factors. Because the reasons are so personal, opinions on the right to bear arms tend to be strong. John Lott, a researcher and gun rights advocate, notes that even "normally level-headed scholars can get very emotional debating guns."[5] A 2016 national poll by NBC News and the *Wall Street Journal* revealed that 50 percent of respondents were concerned that the government may go too far in restricting guns, while 47 percent were concerned that the government would not go far enough in regulation.[6] Those close results indicate that debates over this American value are likely to continue in the future.

DISCUSSION STARTERS

- Why has the right to bear arms become such a debated topic?

- What are alternate views to a strongly progun or a strongly anti-gun position?

- Compare the conditions of contemporary life with those of colonial life. If the founders were to write the Second Amendment today, would they write it the same way?

TIMELINE

1775

In April, colonists fire the first shots of the Revolutionary War at the battles of Lexington and Concord. The first shot would come to be known as "the shot heard round the world" and serve as a symbol connecting arms and independence.

1791

States ratify the Bill of Rights, a list of ten amendments meant to limit the power of the federal government and protect the people's freedoms. The right to bear arms appears in the Second Amendment.

1865

John Wilkes Booth shoots and kills President Abraham Lincoln with a single-bullet pistol.

1868

The Fourteenth Amendment is ratified and becomes part of the US Constitution. The Fourteenth Amendment grants equal protection of the law to all people born or naturalized in the US, including those laws related to the right to bear arms.

1871

Former Union military leaders Colonel William Church and General George Wingate found the National Rifle Association to promote marksmanship skills.

1873

On April 13, a mob of white supremacists disarms and attacks black men guarding a courthouse from political insurrection in Colfax, Louisiana. Dozens of black people were killed in what is now known as the Colfax Massacre.

1876

The Supreme Court offers its first close reading of the Second Amendment in the *Cruikshank* case when it determines that a white man involved in the Colfax Massacre had not violated constitutional rights by disarming the courthouse defenders.

1929

On February 14, the Saint Valentine's Day Massacre draws attention to dangerous weapons.

1934

The 1934 National Firearms Act takes effect as the first major gun control measure enacted by the federal government.

1939

The Supreme Court announces its decision in the *United States v. Miller* case. The court upholds the constitutionality of the 1934 Firearms Act, arguing that regulations against sawed-off shotguns did not violate Second Amendment rights because such weapons bore no connection to service in a militia.

1967

The Black Panthers march at the California state capitol to protest the Mulford Act and assert the right of black people to own guns for self-defense.

1968

In response to recent assassinations of political leaders and black rights activists, the Gun Control Act of 1968 takes effect to regulate interstate gun traffic, strengthen licensing, and prohibit certain kinds of people, such as felons, from obtaining arms.

1977

At its annual meeting, NRA members install new leadership to cement the organization's position as a vocal lobbying group in support of an individual's personal constitutional right to bear arms.

1993

In November, the Brady Act passes with provisions to expand background checks in an effort to keep guns away from mentally ill individuals, such as the man who shot James Brady.

2008

The Supreme Court decides in the case of *District of Columbia v. Heller* that individuals have the right to bear arms for reasons unrelated to service in a militia.

2016

Omar Mateen kills 49 people in a shooting at an Orlando nightclub.

2017

Stephen Paddock kills 58 people in a shooting in Las Vegas.

ESSENTIAL FACTS

THE FREEDOM AND ITS LIMITS

The right to bear arms provides the liberty to own, store, carry, and use firearms. The Second Amendment of the Constitution grants this right. The amendment states, "A well regulated Militia, being necessary to the security of a free State, the right of the people to keep and bear Arms, shall not be infringed." Interpretations of the right focus on different parts of the amendment. Some focus on the second part, viewing the right as a fundamental, individual right. Others focus on the first part, viewing the right to bear arms as a collective right for protection.

This freedom is limited by federal, state, and local laws, as well as by place, personal history, and type of arm. Laws typically do not allow arms in "sensitive places" such as schools and government buildings. In some cases, laws allow people to obtain special licenses or special dispensation to carry arms, openly or concealed, in those places. Laws usually restrict the gun rights of people who have been convicted of a felony or have a history of domestic abuse or mental illness. Furthermore, certain weapons have been banned by law. These include sawed-off shotguns and assault rifles. These bans have changed with time. At various points, in response to various national events and attitudes, bans have been added or have been overturned. In general, bans target weapons that are particularly unusual and dangerous for civilian use.

KEY PLAYERS

- James Madison wrote the text of the Second Amendment, incorporating input and revisions from state representatives.

- Chief Justice Morrison Waite offered a rare, landmark interpretation of the Second Amendment in *United States v. Cruikshank*, arguing that the amendment does nothing more than protect the right to arms from federal infringement. It does not protect the right from individual or state actions.

- William Church and George Wingate founded the National Rifle Association to train young men in marksmanship skills.

- Franklin Roosevelt proposed and signed the National Firearms Act of 1934, the first major attempt at federal gun control.
- John F. Kennedy, Robert F. Kennedy, Malcolm X, Medgar Evers, and Martin Luther King Jr. became the faces of gun violence.
- Bobby Seale and Huey Newton advocated for black armament to defend life and rights during the racially charged violence of the 1960s.
- Sarah and James Brady spurred gun control advocacy efforts to pass legislation expanding background checks.
- Antonin Scalia wrote the opinion for the majority in the pivotal Supreme Court case *District of Columbia v. Heller*. His decision interprets the Second Amendment as an individual right unrelated to service in the militia.

KEY PERSPECTIVES

- Hunting and sports perspective: guns are tools of a craft and as such are to be understood and respected but not feared or vilified.
- Gun rights perspective: guns are essential to safety and liberty, and the government should not interfere with the right to own them.
- Gun control perspective: guns are designed to kill and therefore need to be controlled carefully to protect individuals and society from crimes, accidents, and suicides.
- Compromise perspective: guns have lawful and unlawful purposes. Regulations must preserve the rights of law-abiding citizens but restrict arms access for those who would use them dangerously.

QUOTE

"There's a whole spectrum of gun owners, and I think one of the problems that we have as a country is that there is a very, very narrow view of the gun owner that has a voice."

— *Lily Raff McCaulou*

GLOSSARY

AUTOMATIC WEAPON
A firearm, such as a machine gun, that fires continuously with a single pull of the trigger.

CONCEALED CARRY
Possession of a weapon in public, where the weapon is not readily visible.

DELEGATE
A person sent to a convention to represent a group or a state.

ENVIRONMENTALISM
The support of the improvement, preservation, or restoration of the environment.

HANDGUN
A gun with a barrel less than 12 inches (30 cm) long.

HOMICIDE
The killing of a person by another.

ICONIC
Having the characteristics of someone or something that is very famous or popular.

ILLICIT
Not allowed.

LOBBYIST
Someone who tries to convince government officials to vote in a certain way as part of his or her job.

MINUTEMAN
A member of a militia of American colonists who could be ready at a minute's notice.

OPEN CARRY
Visible possession of a firearm in public.

STIGMA
A mark of dishonor.

STRAW PURCHASE
An illegal gun purchase made by a family member, friend, or acquaintance on behalf of a criminal, juvenile, or other person not legally eligible to buy a firearm.

SUBJUGATE
To bring under control, especially by conquering.

ADDITIONAL RESOURCES

SELECTED BIBLIOGRAPHY

Cornell, Saul. *A Well-Regulated Militia: The Founding Fathers and the Origins of Gun Control in America*. Oxford UP, 2008. Print.

Davidson, Osha Gray. *Under Fire: The NRA and the Battle for Gun Control*. U of Iowa P, 1993.

Dougherty, Kevin. *Weapons of Mississippi*. U of Mississippi P, 2010. Print.

Lansford, Tom. "African Americans and Gun Violence." *Guns in American Society: An Encyclopedia of History, Politics, Culture, and the Law*. Ed. Gregg Lee Carter. 2nd ed. 1 vols. ABC-CLIO, 2012. Print.

Lott, John R., Jr. *More Guns, Less Crime: Understanding Crime and Gun Control Laws*. 3rd ed., U of Chicago P, 2010. Print.

FURTHER READINGS

Hand, Carol. *Gun Control and the Second Amendment*. Minneapolis, MN: Abdo, 2017. Print.

Waldman, Michael. *The Second Amendment: A Biography*. New York: Simon, 2014. Print.

ONLINE RESOURCES

Booklinks
NONFICTION NETWORK
FREE! ONLINE NONFICTION RESOURCES

To learn more about the right to bear arms, visit **abdobooklinks.com**. These links are routinely monitored and updated to provide the most current information available.

MORE INFORMATION

For more information on this subject, contact or visit the following organizations:

BRADY CAMPAIGN TO PREVENT GUN VIOLENCE

840 First Street NE, Suite 400
Washington, DC 20002
202-370-8101

bradycampaign.org

The Brady Campaign to Prevent Gun Violence advocates for gun control. It provides public service campaigns, education outreach initiatives, and research to inform gun policy.

NATIONAL CONSTITUTION CENTER

Independence Mall
525 Arch Street
Philadelphia, PA 19106
215-409-6600

constitutioncenter.org

The National Constitution Center is a nonpartisan institution formed by Congress to inspire curiosity about and understanding of the US Constitution. The center spreads information through interactive exhibits, debates, seminars, discussions, and digital material.

NATIONAL RIFLE ASSOCIATION OF AMERICA

11250 Waples Mill Road
Fairfax, VA 22030
800-672-3888

nra.org

The National Rifle Association is a gun rights advocacy group. It sponsors safety training, educational programs, lobbyist efforts, and research on issues relevant to the right to bear arms.

SOURCE NOTES

CHAPTER 1. DIFFERENT PERSPECTIVES

1. Kevin Dougherty. *Weapons of Mississippi*. Jackson, MS: U of Mississippi P, 2010. Print.

2. John Hayes. "Of Firearms and Family: How Hunters Revere Tradition." *Pittsburgh Post-Gazette*. PG Publishing Company, 29 Nov. 2014. Web. 27 Sept. 2017.

3. "The Bill of Rights." *National Archives*. US National Archives and Records Administration, n.d. Web. 27 Sept. 2017.

4. Scott Willoughby. "Colorado's Hunters Overlooked in Gun Control Debate." *Denver Post*. Digital First Media, 12 Mar. 2013. Web. 27 Sept. 2017.

5. "Gun Violence Task Force Report." *Richard R. Boykin*. Richard Boykin, 14 Dec. 2016. Web. 27 Sept. 2017.

6. Miles Bryan. "Gun Deaths in Chicago Reach Startling Number as Year Closes." *NPR*. NPR, 28 Dec. 2016. Web. 27 Sept. 2017.

7. William Lee. "Fourteen-Year-Old Boy Killed Helping Father Move Out of Apartment," *Chicago Tribune*. Tronc, 29 Oct. 2016. Web. 27 Sept. 2017.

8. Phil Gast. "Oklahoma Mom Calling 911 Asks If Shooting an Intruder Is Allowed." *CNN*. Cable News Network, 4 Jan. 2012. Web. 27 Sept. 2017.

9. John R. Lott, Jr. *More Guns, Less Crime: Understanding Crime and Gun Control Laws*. Chicago, IL: U of Chicago P, 2010. Print.

10. Hannah Fingerhut. "5 Facts about Guns in the United States." *Pew Research Center*. Pew Research Center, 5 Jan. 2016. Web. 27 Sept. 2017.

11. "Cayman Naib." *Sayenough*. Brady Campaign to Prevent Gun Violence, n.d. Web. 27 Sept. 2017.

12. "Suicide and Self-Inflicted Injury." *Centers for Disease Control and Prevention*. US Department of Health & Human Services, 17 Mar. 2017. Web. 27 Sept. 2017.

13. Kenneth D. Kochanek, Sherry L. Murphy, Jiaquan Xu, and Betzaida Tejada-Vera. "Deaths: Final Data for 2014." *Centers for Disease Control and Prevention*. US Department of Health & Human Services, 30 June 2016. Web. 27 Sept. 2017.

14. Madeline Drexler. "Guns & Suicide: The Hidden Toll." *Harvard Public Health*. President and Fellows of Harvard College, n.d. Web. 27 Sept. 2017.

15. Kenneth D. Kochanek, Sherry L. Murphy, Jiaquan Xu, and Betzaida Tejada-Vera. "Deaths: Final Data for 2014." *Centers for Disease Control and Prevention*. US Department of Health & Human Services, 30 June 2016. Web. 27 Sept. 2017.

16. "Arlyn, 18." *Brady Center to Prevent Gun Violence*. Brady Campaign to Prevent Gun Violence, n.d. Web. 27 Sept. 2017.

CHAPTER 2. ARMING A NEW NATION

1. Ralph Waldo Emerson. "Concord Hymn." *Poetry Foundation*. Poetry Foundation, n.d. Web. 27 Sept. 2017.

2. John Ferling. *Whirlwind: The American Revolution and the War That Won It*. New York: Bloomsbury, 2015. Print.

3. "Virginia Declaration of Rights." *Yale Law School*. Lillian Goldman Law Library, n.d. Web. 27 Sept. 2017.

4. "Massachusetts Constitution." *Fundamental Documents*. U of Chicago, n.d. Web. 27 Sept. 2017.

5. Stephen P. Halbrook. *The Founders' Second Amendment: Origins of the Right to Bear Arms*. Chicago, IL: Ivan R. Dee, 2008. Print.

6. David E. Vandercoy. "The History of the Second Amendment." *Valparaiso University Law Review*. Bepress, Spring 1994. Web. 27 Sept. 2017.

CHAPTER 3. RACE AND ARMS RIGHTS POST-CIVIL WAR

1. Ralph A. Rossum. *American Constitutional Law: The Bill of Rights*. Boulder, CO: Westview, 2017. Print.

2. Robert J. Spitzer. *Gun Control a Documentary and Reference Guide*. Greenwood, CT: Greenwood, 2009. Print.

3. James Gray Pope. "Snubbed Landmark: Why United States v. Cruikshank (1876) Belongs at the Heart of the American Constitutional Canon." *Harvard Civil Rights—Civil Liberties Law Review*. Harvard Civil Rights—Civil Liberties Law Review, Spring 2014. Web. 27 Sept. 2017.

4. "Dred Scott's Fight for Freedom." *PBS*. PBS, n.d. Web. 27 Sept. 2017.

5. Eugene Volokh. "Supreme Court Cases on the Right to Bear Arms." *UCLA Law School*. Regents of the U of California, n.d. Web. 27 Sept. 2017.

CHAPTER 4. THE NATIONAL RIFLE ASSOCIATION

1. "A Brief History of the NRA." *National Rifle Association*. NRA, n.d. Web. 28 Sept. 2017.

2. J. Lee Thompson. *Theodore Roosevelt Abroad: Nature, Empire, and the Journey of an American President*. New York: Macmillan, 2013. Print.

3. Theodore Roosevelt. *Outdoor Pastimes of an American Hunter*. Birmingham, AL: Palladium, 1999. Print.

4. Osha Gray Davidson. *Under Fire: the NRA and the Battle for Gun Control*. New York: Holt, 1993. Print.

5. Emily Rupertus. "A Good Guy with a Gun." *National Rifle Association*. NRA, 20 July 2016. Web. 28 Sept. 2017.

6. Michael Waldman. *The Second Amendment: A Biography*. New York: Simon, 2015. Print.

7. Ibid.

8. Osha Gray Davidson. *Under Fire: The NRA and the Battle for Gun Control*. New York: Holt, 1993. Print.

9. Robert J. Spitzer. *The Politics of Gun Control*. Boulder, CO: Paradigm, 2015. Print.

10. Jill Lepore. "Battleground America." *New Yorker*. Condé Nast, 23 Apr. 2012. Web. 28 Sept. 2017.

11. Ibid.

12. "About Us." *Coalition to Stop Gun Violence*. Coalition to Stop Gun Violence, n.d. Web. 28 Sept. 2017.

SOURCE NOTES CONTINUED

CHAPTER 5. POLITICS AND ARMS RIGHTS IN THE 1960S

1. Coretta Scott King. "10 Commandments on Vietnam." *American Rhetoric*. American Rhetoric, 27 Apr. 1968. Web. 28 Sept. 2017.

2. "History of the Black Panther Party: Black Panther Party Platform and Program." *Stanford University*. Stanford University, n.d. Web. 28 Sept. 2017.

3. Joshua Bloom. *Black against Empire: The History and Politics of the Black Panther Party*. Berkeley, CA: U of California P, 2013. Print

4. Ibid.

5. "What We Do." *Bureau of Alcohol, Tobacco, Firearms and Explosives*. US Department of Justice, n.d. Web. 28 Sept. 2017.

6. Adam Winkler. *Gunfight: The Battle Over the Right to Bear Arms in America*. New York: Norton, 2011. Print.

CHAPTER 6. THE BRADY CAMPAIGN

1. Duke Today Staff. "Has the Brady Act Been Successful?" *Duke Today*. Duke University, 1 Sept. 2000. Web. 28 Sept. 2017.

2. "Brady Law." *Bureau of Alcohol, Tobacco, Firearms and Explosives*. US Department of Justice, 28 Apr. 2017. Web. 28 Sept. 2017.

3. "About Brady." *Brady Campaign to Prevent Gun Violence*. Brady Campaign to Prevent Gun Violence, n.d. Web. 28 Sept. 2017.

4. Scott H. Decker. Susan Pennell, and Ami Caldwell. "Illegal Firearms: Access and Use by Arrestees." *National Institute of Justice*. US Department of Justice, Jan. 1997. Web. 28 Sept. 2017.

5. "Keep Crime Guns Off Our Streets." *Brady Campaign to Prevent Gun Violence*. Brady Campaign to Prevent Gun Violence, n.d. Web. 28 Sept. 2017.

6. "About Brady." *Brady Campaign to Prevent Gun Violence*. Brady Campaign to Prevent Gun Violence, n.d. Web. 28 Sept. 2017.

7. "Statistics." *National Coalition against Domestic Violence*. NCADV, n.d. Web. 28 Sept. 2017.

8. "Guns and Violence against Women." *Everytown for Gun Safety*. Everytown for Gun Safety Support Fund, n.d. Web. 28 Sept. 2017.

CHAPTER 7. INDIVIDUAL RIGHTS AND SELF-DEFENSE

1. "Justice Scalia, Opinion of the Court." *Cornell University Law School*. Cornell University Law School, 26 June 2008. Web. 28 Sept. 2017.

2. George Yancy and Janine Jones, ed. *Pursuing Trayvon Martin: Historical Contexts and Contemporary Manifestations of Racial Dynamics*. Lanham, MD: Lexington, 2013.

3. "Stevens, J., Dissenting." *Cornell University Law School*. Cornell University Law School, 26 June 2008. Web. 28 Sept. 2017.

4. "Syllabus." *Cornell University Law School*. Cornell University Law School, n.d. Web. 28 Sept. 2017.

5. Michael Waldman. *The Second Amendment: A Biography*. New York: Simon, 2015. Print.

6. Ben Romans. "Supreme Court Justices Kagan and Scalia Are Hunting Partners." *Field & Stream*. Field & Stream, 5 July 2013. Web. 28 Sept. 2017.

7. "Stevens, J., Dissenting." *Cornell University Law School*. Cornell University Law School, 26 June 2008. Web. 28 Sept. 2017.

CHAPTER 8. MASS SHOOTINGS AND MENTAL HEALTH

1. Yuval Neria, Sandro Galea, Fran H. Norris, ed. *Mental Health and Disasters*. Cambridge, UK: Cambridge UP, 2009. Print.

2. William J. Krouse and Daniel J. Richardson. "Mass Murder with Firearms: Incidents and Victims, 1999–2013." *Congressional Research Service*. Federation of American Scientists, 30 July 2015. Web. 28 Sept. 2017.

3. "Fourteen Persons Wounded." *Daily Alta California* 31 Mar. 1891: 1. *California Digital Newspaper Collection*. Web. 13 Oct. 2017.

4. Melanie Burney. "Survivor Looks Back in Anger on 1949 Massacre." *Los Angeles Times*. Los Angeles Times, 3 Oct. 1999. Web. 28 Sept. 2017.

5. Associated Press. "Beginning of an Era: The 1966 University of Texas Clock Tower Shooting." *NBC News*. NBC News, 1 Aug. 2016. Web. 28 Sept. 2017.

6. Colleen L. Barry, Emma E. McGinty, Jon S. Vernick, and Daniel W. Webster. "After Newton—Public Opinion on Gun Policy and Mental Illness." *New England Journal of Medicine*. Massachusetts Medical Society, 28 Jan. 2013. Web. 28 Sept. 2017.

7. Jonathan M. Metzl and Kenneth T. MacLeish. "Mental Illness, Mass Shootings, and the Politics of American Firearms." *American Journal of Public Health* 105.2 (2015): 240–249. Print.

8. Ben Agger and Timothy W. Luke, ed. *Gun Violence and Public Life*. Boulder, CO: Paradigm, 2014. Print.

9. Helen Gavin. *Female Aggression*. Chichester, West Sussex: Wiley-Blackwell, 2015. Print.

CHAPTER 9. THE FUTURE OF THE RIGHT TO BEAR ARMS

1. Lily Raff McCaulou. "Hunters Need to Stop Letting the NRA Speak for Them." *Atlantic*. Atlantic Monthly Group, 11 Jan. 2013. Web. 28 Sept. 2017.

2. "A Hunter on Gun Control: 'We Want Something to Change.'" *NPR*. NPR, 3 Oct. 2015. Web. 28 Sept. 2017.

3. "Justice Scalia, Opinion of the Court." *Cornell University Law School*. Cornell University Law School, 26 June 2008. Web. 28 Sept. 2017.

4. Ibid.

5. John R. Lott Jr. *More Guns, Less Crime: Understanding Crime and Gun Control Laws*. Chicago, IL: U of Chicago P, 2010. Print.

6. Carrie Dann. "Poll: Voters Divided on Government Role in Gun Control, Access." *NBC News*. NBC News, 26 June 2016. Web. 28 Sept. 2017.

INDEX

ABOUT THE AUTHORS

DUCHESS HARRIS, JD, PHD

Professor Harris is the chair of the American Studies Department at Macalester College. The author and coauthor of four books (*Hidden Human Computers: The Black Women of NASA* and *Black Lives Matter* with Sue Bradford Edwards, *Racially Writing the Republic: Racists, Race Rebels, and Transformations of American Identity* with Bruce Baum, and *Black Feminist Politics from Kennedy to Clinton/Obama*), she has been an associate editor for *Litigation News*, the American Bar Association Section's quarterly flagship publication, and was the first editor-in-chief of *Law Raza Journal*, an interactive online race and the law journal for William Mitchell College of Law.

She has earned a PhD in American Studies from the University of Minnesota and a Juris Doctorate from William Mitchell College of Law.

REBECCA MORRIS

Rebecca Morris has a PhD in English from Texas A&M University. She is coeditor of *Representing Children in Chinese and US Children's Literature* (Ashgate, 2014), a contributor to *Jacqueline Wilson* (ed. Lucy Pearson, Palgrave Macmillan New Casebooks, 2015), and the author of nonfiction books for students. Morris also writes for several educational websites.